The 5 Buckets

A Framework for Living with Intention

BY BOBBY DYSART

THINK TWICE
BOOKS

THINK TWICE

B O O K S

SPECIAL SALES

Think Twice books are available at a special discount for bulk purchases for sales promotions or corporate training programs. Special editions, including personalized covers and custom forewords, are also available. For more details, email info@thinktwice.com or contact the author directly.

To all of us looking for a little guidance.

Thank you to Jennifer, Liz, Ela, Rohit, Ashley and my wonderful wife, Tracy.

CONTENTS

Original cover art designed by Lisa Taranchenko

DON'T WAIT. START SMALL. LEARN AS YOU GO.

The Magic

It's a mystical power just within our reach
Tough to master but easy to teach
Like words that form after writing for hours
A strange voice surfaces we know isn't ours

We must nurture The Magic so not to waste
Effort and dedication what it craves to taste
It grows from listening, reading and waking
Available to us all, it's ours for the taking

The challenge lies in its resistance to idle
It only shows when we put in our miles
Have faith The Magic always comes about
It also sees precisely what we put out

The Magic can't be fooled and it does not play
It notices when we miss just a couple days
Commitment, one of The Magic's strongest fuels
Test this truth and you see The Magic can be cruel

Fear not, The Magic can be forgiving too
It has a way of getting just enough out of you
Forgiveness is another piece of The Magic's puzzle
Let things pass and you'll have no trouble

Magic comes most easily with one simple action
Turns out love is The Magic's greatest attraction
So pour love out for the world to soak up
You'll have magic to fill even the deepest of cups

INTRODUCTION

I wrote that poem in May of 2020. Like many people, I was in a tough place. Only ten months into my second business, I lost over half my clients in the same week. Memories of closing my first business surfaced. I was scared it was happening again. The fear of failure draped over me like a weighted cloak. I retreated to my office, engulfed in apprehension and indecision.

I would hide there for hours, my laptop screen staring back at me. I slowly eked out blemished work stained by hours of negative thoughts, late nights and my partnership with alcohol. It was a bad friendship, I found comfort in hazy IPAs and a hefty dose of CNN. I was glued to screens: television, computer, phone... whatever would take my mind off the potential of failure. I was adrift. I gave more hours to my work for nothing more than giving hours to my work. It was a monotonous dream state where I limped through my life for two months.

Then I woke up. Literally, around five AM on a Saturday morning, I rose from my slumber. I thought about commitment. Commitment had fueled many good things in my life: my parents' marriage, my marriage, my success in business, my wrestling career, etc. I wrote that poem that Saturday morning, knowing I had channeled a little genius. Thankfully, it drove me to explore myself and the other areas of my life.

When I first moved to Southern California in 2007, I had one driving ambition: live near the Pacific Ocean. It wasn't the loftiest of goals but hey, I grew up in suburban Ohio. I wanted to stick my feet in the sand, hear the crashing waves and smell the salt-filled air. I wanted to wear flip-flops in December. And I wanted these things woven into my everyday life. I remember feeling spoiled each time I sat on the beach. It was pure bliss.

After a few years, my motivation shifted squarely to my career. I focused on getting a general management position at my first employer. Then building a web startup with a friend. Then climbing the ladder at a software company. Then at another. Chasing bumps in salary and Director, VP and CRO titles. Finally, I started my own consulting business.

During each stint, I obsessed over my next commission, promotion or opportunity. I hopelessly focused on reaching the next level of success or hitting some moving target of satisfaction.

Even while running my business, I was either dwelling on the day I would lose it all or fixating on the day when millions of dollars would roll in. The day when I would feel whole.

The morning I wrote that poem, I felt more whole than I had in years. Getting words out of my head and onto paper, sorting through what I was trying to say, working to nail the messaging, sound and flow, all made me feel incredibly fulfilled. Then I went for a run. I cruised out the door in my Nikes headed toward the pier nearby. Melodic house music streamed from my phone into my ears. I gasped for air, staring at the sunrise in the distance. Once I hit the end of the boardwalk, I stopped to take it all in. No fears consumed my mind. No thoughts of making more money or building a bigger, better business cluttered my consciousness. Just me, enjoying every exhausted breath while the day unfolded.

From that morning forward, I noticed minor changes in how I approached my days. I woke up earlier. I began writing more. I went for walks outside and rode my bike. I watched less television and read more books. I had increased curiosity and decreased anxiety. I found pleasure in process: slicing a pineapple, preparing tea or reading before bed.

I developed a deeper connection with my daily actions.

I didn't know it yet, but that was the beginning of my discovery of The 5 Buckets. I was living with more intention.

A few months later, my good friend Kenny invited me to a men's retreat. I respect Kenny and his invitation delighted me. Without asking many questions, I committed and joined the weekend retreat in Idyllwild, California.

The event centered on personal growth. Twenty of us engaged in physical, mental and collaborative challenges. It was an awesome experience where I met some wonderful people. While we each had many takeaways, the practice of setting intentions and being present struck me most. I found myself slowing down and using all my senses to fully experience each moment.

The retreat was very ceremonial. We participated in yoga, breathwork, meditation, creative and sharing sessions. We challenged ourselves by plunging into ice baths for three-minute intervals. We did group workouts and enjoyed meals together. It all had a bit of formality to it. There were introductions before sharing circles, chants during breathwork and prayers of gratitude after the ice baths. Everything was scheduled but never rushed. There was a clear beginning and end with plenty of time to transition. A weekend had never passed by with more perfect pace.

During one meditation ceremony, I caught myself humming along to a song played by Charles, one of the group leaders. He strummed a guitar and performed the song, "I Pure" by Franko Heke. It is a spiritual song, almost religious. I had never heard it before but immediately felt moved by it.

Charles sang the words, "I pray for guidance." He repeated the phrase a few times throughout the song. The word "guidance" struck me. It triggered instant emotion. I teared up then broke down in a sort of relief. I realized in that moment, I was and had been in search of guidance. Moreover, I was looking for some reassurance regarding how I was living my life. I hadn't previously known that was something I wanted or needed (at least not consciously). Remember, I committed to this event essentially on a whim. So I was surprised by my emotion and the impact of the moment. I cried. I smiled. I reflected. I was grateful for my realization. Something deep inside me had been revealed and I was eager to explore my new understanding.

We were urged to write things down as ideas and memories came to us throughout the retreat. As I sat there in relief, my blank pages began to fill. I felt compelled to capture my thoughts on paper. I wrote:

Guidance is what I am looking for.
Guidance led me to being present.
Indulge in the challenge of focusing on each moment.

I didn't totally understand what I meant but that word "indulge" felt right. If I was going to embrace this challenge, I needed a way to organize myself. I thought, "What areas of my life are most important?" Five came to mind: relationships, creativity, health, learning and work. I wrote them down then thought about what focusing on each area might look like on a weekly basis. If I could prioritize several moments or intentions ahead of time then perhaps I could learn to enjoy each for what they were. I would name three intentions across the five categories (or buckets as the group called them) each week. If I could do this consistently, I would learn to focus on each moment and find my guidance.

The formalities of each ceremony, the pace of the weekend, the thoughtfulness put into each moment and my own need for guidance all served to organize The 5 Buckets framework in my mind. I found myself immediately sharing my discovery with anyone who would listen. It started at the retreat where I began telling the group that a framework around five buckets had come to me during one of our sessions. During my drive home, I called to tell my wife, parents and a few friends. I was surprised by my own excitement as well as the validation and curiosity of those I told. Upon my return home, I immediately began practicing The 5 Buckets.

Increasing intention in my life was initially a selfish act. I needed it. It filled a gap in my being that had existed for a long time. I found more appreciation for the people, responsibilities and opportunities in my life. I was more thoughtful in my decisions and aware of my actions. I stopped drinking. I cooked and prepared healthy food. I lost fifteen pounds. I told my wife, Tracy, "I know this sounds crazy but I think I lost mental weight." She laughed and I shrugged. The weight remains off and I stand by that initial observation.

The biggest shift was my reconnection to writing. I wrote more consistently in those first couple months than I had ever before. And future achievement or notoriety wasn't driving me. I just wanted to put pen to paper. I rediscovered my love for the practice. When sharing the shift with friends, they rightfully questioned what created the change. The truth is, it was a long time coming. Thousands of words hid inside my head and on my phone's notepad. Writing had always spilled out of me. But I capped and stored it more often than not.

You are reading this text because quickly I felt compelled to help others experience what I was experiencing. Practicing The 5 Buckets paves me a road toward purpose.

My purpose is to find meaning in my every day and expand that meaning through writing, sharing and learning more.

I write for purpose. I write for meaning. I write for you and for me. It is all well aligned.

If you take nothing else from this book, take stock in what makes you feel whole and set yourself up to experience it consistently; experience it fully. You'll find new things to appreciate each time. My first days living by the Pacific were thirteen years ago. I am not sure I have lived with that much intention since. I walked to the beach to feel the sun. I waded into the water to feel the waves crash against my body. Each time, I discovered another sense of gratitude. Life's treasures are always there, both hidden and obvious, just waiting for us to enjoy.

THE 5 BUCKETS

The core purpose of this book is to help us live with more balance and intention. By naming, organizing and completing intentions consistently, we improve our chances of actualizing the life we desire. The 5 Buckets framework simply provides an effective medium.

Each day, we face an unprecedented amount of distractions. Phones, emails, television, advertisements, social media, friends, family, acquaintances and more exhaust our attention. Each represents a challenge to our ability to live intentionally. Out of necessity, we seek the paths of least resistance as opposed to the paths we most want to follow. We are being pulled through our lives one interruption, notification and message at a time. And these are only the external components.

Our own minds pose even greater challenges to our intention. They race from thought to thought in an endless loop. More information, more gratification, more possessions, more experiences, more validation and more drama. If we aren't thinking about tomorrow, then we are dwelling on yesterday. If we aren't asking, "What if?" then we are asking, "What could have been?" We spend loads of energy contemplating life's big questions instead of relishing life's small moments. The latter is a much more fulfilling approach.

If gaining control of all our thoughts sounds like a daunting task, it is! I argue it is impossible. What is possible is improving our awareness and clarity. We become aware of our distractions and clarify how we want to spend our time. As a result, we are given the massive opportunity to live out the lives we want. We savor each wonderful moment. We explore the world as we see fit.

We map our life's purpose and enjoy the ride.

The 5 Buckets provides that map and you provide the compass. I share my experience for additional perspective and connection. The real education comes from you experiencing your personal journey with the framework. Living with intention lets The Universe know what you want. And as you learned long ago, actions speak louder than words.

> # "When you came into this world so did the world come out of you."
>
> —Griz, "No Time Like The Present"

In the pages that follow, we briefly review the following areas of our lives:

Relationships
Creativity
Health
Learning
Work

In each section, I describe the purpose and correlation of each area as it relates to this framework. I also share insights regarding my personal experiences using the framework. To help you begin, I break down using The 5 Buckets into three actions: *Plan, Complete and Reflect.*

PLAN

Each week, set aside at least thirty minutes to think through your intentions. I usually do this on Sunday afternoon. It is important not to rush. Enjoy the time you commit to the practice. I often make myself a cup of tea to complement my planning session. It slows me down and helps me focus.

There is an Intention Guide included at the end of the book that mimics how I organize my intentions. There you can record three per bucket to schedule and complete in a given week.

An intention is a planned moment
you want to experience.

The description you choose to describe each intention can be as brief or thorough as necessary. It is your opportunity to identify what moments you want to experience during your week of life.

I recommend starting with the Relationship Bucket. Begin by considering relationships you want to invest in. Who do you want to reconnect with? Who would you like to learn something from? Who might appreciate hearing from you? Write the names of three people. If you already have plans with someone, you may include that person's name as one of the three. There is no reason to overlook interactions you are already choosing to prioritize.

Next, think of simple ways to connect with your three relationships. Perhaps you want to call one of them and schedule coffee with another. Just planning a quick text to mom or dad can serve as a great start for the Relationship Bucket. You might also send someone a small gift like a card or flowers—anything to remind them you are thinking of them. I'll share more about relationships in the next chapter. After naming your three relationship intentions, move to recording the rest. One bucket at a time.

I go in the following order: Relationships, Creativity, Health, Learning then Work. It is important to think through each bucket carefully. Fostering new and deepening current relationships is vital to living with intention. Our friends, family, partners and acquaintances support, shape and guide us. Care for your people and they'll care for you. Creativity is a powerful and often neglected skill. It needs to be fed and nurtured. Write, draw, color, act, play, cook, dance... it all works. Your health plays a critical role in how you maximize your intentioned life. A clear mind and able body serve as the vehicles for your journey. Learning provides you with perspective regarding how you want to live your life and better serve your purpose. Finally, your work is your contribution. What treasure do you want to offer the world? Regardless of the work you do, you better serve yourself and others by being thoughtful and intentional in your approach.

The key is to start small and get intentions down on paper. And if that means you only get five or ten down to start, then so be it. Just taking the time to name a few intentions is a valuable practice. And as you begin, I reiterate the smaller, the better. Perhaps you start with a few intentions you think you will do anyway, like going to the gym, making dinner or leading a work call. Wherever you begin, make each intention tangible and initially, fairly easy to complete. This sets you up for success as you use the framework. Success in this context means finding awareness and value in even the smallest, most mundane of moments. There is plenty of time to tackle planning and enjoying more creative ones.

After recording your intentions, schedule time to complete them in your calendar. Spread them out over the entire week and remain mindful of how long you want to commit to each. Some may only take a few minutes and others may take hours. Allow for time to transition between intentions and anything else you might have scheduled. Use the weekends and early morning. I find these times to be particularly useful for creativity, health and learning intentions.

COMPLETE

As we use The 5 Buckets, understand we are not trying to create habits. More precisely, we are developing a practice of living intentionally. We develop this practice by planning and completing intentions throughout our days and weeks. We cleanse our schedule of moments not serving us and prioritize moments we value and deem important to living our lives. We learn what comes easy, what we skip or reschedule, and how we experience each intention.

Our aim is to realize the uniqueness of each moment and experience it fully.

In completing each intention, keep in mind the value of the experience or journey; the act of completion itself. I am all too often focused on an outcome or a destination. Completing intentions using The 5 Buckets has helped me find more value in experience itself.

For The Health Bucket, don't think, "I want to start running." Instead, write the intention, "Jog to Sunset Ridge Park." Then enjoy that jog, on that day, in that moment for what it is. Perhaps you do it again the following week, or maybe you never jog to Sunset Ridge Park again. Either way, it does not matter. What does matter is, for that moment, you prioritized one intention over the millions of items competing for your time and attention.

Take it a step further by indulging in that specific moment. Notice the entire experience. Admire the sun's rays stretching across the massive sky.

Stomp through shallow puddle ponds while jogging in the rain. Listen to the cars drive by while running through the busy city streets. Embrace the silence of the suburban neighborhood sidewalks early in the morning. Feel the wind's resistance or race freely down the hill. Whatever the situation, find gratitude and appreciate the moment's entirety.

As you complete intentions, notice your increased awareness. When I began using The 5 Buckets, I realized a distinct difference in my awareness of my week's happenings. I initially front-loaded my schedule with intentions, hoping to complete a majority in the first few days. I slotted several back-to-back and missed my scheduled times repeatedly. Work meetings ran long, unexpected phone calls rang and everyday chores sucked up my time. I did not shame myself, nor was I disappointed. I noted each miss, rescheduled for later in the week and found gratification in understanding how the week's plan was changing. Just knowing what intentions were slipping away provided me helpful information. I didn't realize it but I was practicing a key component: Reflection.

REFLECT

One definition of reflection by Merriam-Webster reads, "consideration of some subject matter, idea or purpose." As a person who prides myself on action, taking time to consider purpose, results and takeaways from my actions can be challenging. My default mindset is to keep moving and find more ways to contribute. However, taking even brief amounts of time to reflect on my experience using The 5 Buckets has proven to be both beneficial and necessary.

As an intention within my Relationship Bucket, I jumped on a video call with a new friend, Sean. We had scheduled time to review a side project he was considering. Sean is intelligent, driven and passionate about the idea behind the project. However, he was questioning the best way to get started. After sorting through his options out loud, we settled on immediate next steps and an efficient path to launch. While he came away excited and praised me with credit, he did the heavy lifting and was going to have to execute the plan. He had all the answers and I had simply asked some helpful questions. Afterward, I took stock on my experience. I noticed I had come away with loads of energy. I was exploding with ideas and momentum to continue sharing with him as well as to take into my own work. I immediately wrote this down. Helping Sean clearly had a dramatic effect on me, and I wanted to replicate that effect.

I also completed many reflections that led to me writing this book. As I mentioned, I began sharing The 5 Buckets with anyone and everyone the moment I wrote the concept down during that retreat in Idyllwild. I told friends, family, colleagues, new acquaintances... anyone who would listen.

As I did, I began asking myself questions:

Why am I so excited about this?
How has this story evolved?
What more am I learning?
What am I avoiding?

The more I asked myself these questions, the more I wrote. I began recording the nuances of what I was learning by using this framework. I realized how my thoughts on the framework and its benefits progressed. I captured others' reactions and ideas on my phone's notepad. I fed my growing curiosity. Finally, there came a point where I noticed my lessons were too great for a quick, verbal share. I felt compelled to move the concept forward and decided to write this book.

You can't expect yourself to always reflect in the ways I just described. Taking time to analyze and understand your experiences is challenging. To increase your periods of reflection, add two components to your weekly planning. As you draft your intentions, record an observation regarding three intentions from your previous week. Also record a count of how many intentions you completed compared to the fifteen you named.

See the Weekly Reflection section of the included Intention Guide for additional reference.

Here is a sample of my own reflections:

13/15 (count)

I got a ton of value from my interactions with Ryan. His perspective on running small experiments to build skills for larger opportunities resonated. Remember he's coming to Long Beach next month and we should connect while he's in LA.

My first mountain bike ride kicked my butt! I remember feeling challenged physically and mentally. While it frustrated me at times, I felt great getting through it to the end. When back home, I should call Finn to schedule time to go with him since I know he does it often.

Tuesday morning's writing session was helpful. I brain dumped four pages at six AM. I felt clear and ready for the day afterward. I immediately went for a walk to let the morning unfold. Awesome way to start a day.

As shown, these observations only need to be a few sentences. You gain helpful perspective through this simple exercise.

Take the time to remember how the week played out. You might also ask yourself questions like, "What did I enjoy most about a certain intention?" and "What did I most avoid?" Reflection is personal, so figure out what works best for you and run with it.

> # "A defining condition of being human is that we have to understand the meaning of our experience."
>
> —Jack Mezirow, *Transformative Dimensions of Adult Learning*

Plan, complete and reflect.

Doing so for just one week provides knowledge and enjoyment. You have a clear process along with a guide to record your experience. You understand the challenges of distractions and rewards for using this framework. You have seen examples of how I use The 5 Buckets to gain awareness and clarity.

You are that much closer to living with intention. I invite you to begin.

Above all else, begin.

LIVING WITH INTENTION

Once you balance important areas of your life and deliberately invest in each, you find answers to life's big questions. I answer them for myself each time I write. Each time I wake up early and make myself tea. Each time I run on the beach. Each time I read Julia Cameron. Each time I put a website together. Each time I put myself out there for a new friend to find. When I do these things I stumble across my purpose, and complementary forces show up to aid my efforts.

Around May of 2019, I reached out to an acquaintance from college. His name is Kevin. After college, Kevin moved east and I west. We lost touch but crossed paths every once in a while on LinkedIn. We enjoyed catching up over a phone call after a long absence. I was building my consulting business and thought Kevin might have interest. After the call, we kept in touch and worked on a few projects together.

When I mentioned I was writing this book, Kevin suggested I connect with another transplant, Tom. Tom moved from Ohio to California.

He also self-published three books.

Tom and I hit it off right away. He loved what I was writing and offered his help. He mentioned he felt compelled to *pay it forward*. Many aided his efforts as he produced his books. He could help with self-publishing and marketing. He also introduced me to Jennifer.

Jennifer is an editor and a poet. I looked her up when Tom mentioned he would introduce us. The first thing I read was her framework for putting together poetry collections. Then came our introductory call. I summarized The 5 Buckets. The story resonated. She was reading Eckhart Tolle's, *A New Earth*. I thought to myself, "I am meeting an editor, who is a poet and also studying intention? I am in the right place."

In his book, *The Power of Intention*, Dr. Wayne Dyer refers to intention as the creative force from which all things reach their fullest potential. He describes it as the same force that wills the massive oak tree out of a tiny acorn. The same force that helped Thomas Edison see light where there was darkness. He also mentions we must show up in ways to work alongside intention and not against it.

He writes, "You get what you intend to create by being in harmony with the power of intention, which is responsible for all of creation." Dr. Dyer explains that this is distinctly different from getting what we want. If we focus on what we want, the power of intention leaves us in our state of wanting.

As I practice The 5 Buckets, I sense the creative energy the doctor references. It manifests itself through relationships like those with Tom and Jennifer. My body and mind feel it. I sense it is the energy waking me up before five in the morning. My alarm is set for six but I consistently wake earlier. As I write this sentence, I recall waking even earlier, called to the books and journals fueling my work.

Steven Pressfield mentions this same creative force in his book, *The Artist's Journey*:

> **"It operates in real time and in the real world. It is connected to forces unconstrained by time and space, by reason or by nature's laws. It is capable of summoning allies and assistance and of concentrating them on your behalf and in your cause. These forces are not only of the imagination - ideas, insights, wisdom, breakthroughs in your life and work - but also practical and material apparitions like friends and allies, connections, places to stay, money."**

Steven also mentions a daemon. That we all have a daemon. A guardian charged with connecting us to creation so we produce our masterpieces. So we grow into oak trees.

We spend our lives resisting our daemon's urging. This resistance causes pain. I felt this pain before writing the first words of The 5 Buckets. As I named my first intentions after the retreat, that pain subsided.

In the same book, Pressfield quotes a passage by James Rhodes written in the *Guardian*:

> *"And only when the pain of not doing it got greater than the imagined pain of doing it did I somehow find the balls to pursue what I really wanted and had been obsessed by since the age of seven - to be a concert pianist."*

James' daemon won him over. It willed him into honing his craft over the next several years. He went on to record six top-selling albums and perform international tours in some of the world's greatest concert halls.

My daemon wants me writing. And I wanted to write a book my entire life. But when I began practicing The 5 Buckets, I wasn't thinking about writing a book. I was after balance, guidance and relief. Remember, I was in pain. Though after six weeks, I began to write this book. My daemon awakened. I felt closely aligned with Dr. Dyer's *power of intention*. I sensed I was aligning with The Universe. I stumbled across my purpose, one intention and one day at a time.

DON'T WAIT. START SMALL. LEARN AS YOU GO.

DON'T WAIT.

In college, I remember outlining a novel called The Carpenter. I framed houses during the day to pay for tuition. Splitting my days between the job site and the classroom seemed like an interesting subject. It was an autobiographical fiction of sorts. I had the climactic ending all planned out.

Then I was going to write a guide for Ohio college grads to move to California, like a handy manual for twenty-somethings looking to leave the Midwest.

I considered putting together a collection of my poetry. I have close to fifty poems hidden in my phone's notepad.

When I turned thirty, I thought about writing a book on all the important crap I learned in my twenties. Things like how to order Subway properly, be a good roommate and not to chase the night.

In thirty-seven years, I didn't write any of those books. I wrote the first draft of this one in only six weeks.

Like many, I waited. Waited for the perfect time. Waited for the right idea. Waited to be ready.

Writing a book is an undertaking. I didn't practice. I waited. I could've spent the last decade writing and would have written plenty of books by now.

I didn't wait to implement The 5 Buckets. Initially, I was sloppy. I jotted my intentions down in my journal. One to three words described each one. I forgot many and rescheduled others. I had no real clue what I was doing.

But I didn't wait.

Quickly, I got in a groove. I enjoyed each experience and got a ton of value from just following through on only a few intentions. I gained momentum. You will do the same.

You are priming your practice.
Your practice to live with intention.

Your practice to be balanced and deliberate.For several weeks, this will be the case. Pay no mind to how well or poorly you think you're doing Just write the intentions down. Plan, complete and reflect.

START SMALL.

Remember, an intention is a planned moment you want to experience. The description you choose to describe each intention can be as brief or thorough as necessary.

The thought of completing fifteen intentions each week overwhelmed my friends and family. Several candidly suggested I shrink the number to only a few. While I listened to each suggestion gratefully, I also thought to myself, "We complete many more activities than fifteen in any given week... we just need a way of prioritizing these activities." With 168 hours available, we can fit in fifteen items we deem important, right?

The key is starting small. An intention can be a quick text to your husband, a walk around the block, three minutes listening to Eckhart Tolle or making a paper airplane with your kid. Length and time do not matter. Again, you are priming your practice.

And if you only get a few on the page, then so be it. You are building. You are learning.

LEARN AS YOU GO.

After only a few weeks of using The 5 Buckets, I noticed several changes in myself.

My energy increased. I have always been a morning person, so I expect energy at sunrise. But I also got creative bursts after dinner or even right before bed. I'd crank out chores that used to drain me, like folding my laundry and putting it away.

I looked forward to things. Odd things. One night, I noticed the warmth of the water as I washed dishes. I noticed it enough to appreciate what I was doing, and I looked forward to the next night I had to do them. It felt soothing and almost comforting. Instead of dreading the activity, I savored it. I had never felt that before.

I found time. Loads of time. Time to walk my dog, Bernie. Time for coffee meetups, Zoom calls and learning to play the ukulele. Time to help Tracy with her taxes. Time to read about writing. Time to practice writing. And time to write... like *write*, write.

All of this I learned as I went along. I didn't expect any of it when I named my first intentions.

I learned what intentions mattered to me, what moments I wanted to experience more often and what I was unwilling to cede to distractions. I realized missed opportunities. I developed a new context for understanding my schedule's relationship to purpose.

Your version of living with intention will take shapes unknown. You will surprise yourself. You will expand the framework in ways no one has ever imagined. That is the point. The framework is an on-ramp. Training wheels. A coloring book. You discover how you want to live.

I remembered how much I love to read, and how much reading helps my creativity and mindset. It helps me show up better in my relationships. And those relationships lead to better work and better health. It all aligns quickly. Momentum in one area affects the others exponentially.

Don't wait. Start small. Learn as you go.

You read this many times in this book and my other content. It is a message to you as well as to myself. I use it daily as a core tool in living with intention.

I began this section sharing how practicing The 5 Buckets brought new relationships into my life. These relationships remain important to me and my work. In the next section, we examine the Relationship Bucket. I organize it first as it is perhaps the most important area of the five.

THE RELATIONSHIP BUCKET

Your intention is:

*To connect. Call that old friend
and text that new acquaintance.*

The world wants to hear from you.

I pull up to a brick building on Pier Avenue in Hermosa Beach. I must have walked by this building one hundred times. I stand on top of a hill overlooking Hermosa's Pier. I stare at the shops and restaurants I visited in my early days living in the South Bay. The beach sits just beyond Hennessey's, the flagship Irish pub I dove into many times in years prior. I wait on my friend Sean to come find me.

The brick building is three stories and serves as office space for half a dozen small businesses. Sean strolls out of an east-facing side door to greet me. He mentions his two-bedroom apartment is located on the back side of the brick building. I had no idea people lived this close to Pier Avenue.

Sean is a new friend. He and I met at the Idyllwild retreat. In my second week practicing The 5 Buckets, I recorded an intention to meet Sean over Zoom. He's a smart, healthy, kind and entrepreneurial person, and I knew immediately I wanted to invest in our relationship.

After walking up a flight of stairs, Sean ushered us through his front door. If positive energy has a smell, it smells like Sean's home. It must be a combination of incense, candles and the Pacific breeze. We take off our shoes and hang a right. We walk through the kitchen, then through a large, glass sliding door. Outside is a massive, rustic wooden deck. We sit two stories up with a panoramic view of Hermosa Beach. Damn, I am glad I made the hour drive up.

Sean asks about the drive, Tracy and my book. He also shares updates on his projects. He is writing a men's journal and building a wellness program for first responders. He works as a Chief Fire Engineer for the LAFD full-time. We wrap up our conversation, put our shoes back on and walk to the pier to grab some lunch.

I buy us a couple burritos and we sit on a boardwalk bench facing the ocean. He tells me he recently hurt his back and he hasn't been working at the fire department the last couple weeks. I can tell it is weighing on him. He is grateful for the extra time to put into the journal and wellness program but desperately wants to return to his team.

Last week, he worried about a rumor going around that he isn't as injured as he claims. He thought he might even know who started the rumor. He thought about confronting the person. Then he noticed that person listed as injured. Instead of confronting the person, he sent a text to check in on him.

Turns out Sean's coworker had a serious case of coronavirus. The virus was killing off his nervous system and he was searching for a trusted neurologist. Sean's dad had worked with an amazing neurologist just a few months prior. Sean was able to coordinate an introduction between the doctor and his coworker.

Talk about a close call. Sean nearly accused this person of spreading rumors about him. Instead, he made an introduction that might've saved the guy's health.

I share this story as an example of how important relationships can be. In this instance, a relationship meant access to a much needed health professional. I learned an important lesson myself and am glad I made the trip. Trips like this one weren't normal for me prior to practicing The 5 Buckets.

Have you ever found yourself at a party, event or gathering only to realize several hours later you spent the entire time speaking to the same person? Perhaps you exchange small talk with a few others but for the most part, you are swallowed up by one particular interaction. I am sure there is some science behind this phenomenon but I want to focus on the impact of this tendency in a broader way. It serves as one example of how we operate our lives at scale.

Without some planning, we tend to interact with the same individuals each day, week, month and year. And this comes at a large cost as our relationships can have the greatest impact on how our lives are shaped. Jim Rohn said, "You are the average of the five people you spend the most time with." My mother mentioned some version of this at least a hundred times during my childhood (and maybe even a hundred times since) but OK, what do we do with this wisdom? If a handbook was ever given out on how to level up my relationships, I did not get a copy.

I deliberately begin with the Relationship Bucket because of its sheer power. Our relationships are the greatest enhancers and strongest detractors present in our lives. If we can only invest in a single bucket, we invest in this bucket. Relationships provide us strength, support and scale. The people we surround ourselves with are our partners in building the lives we want. We have the potential to not only bring people into our lives who can drastically improve them but also keep people at bay who can negatively impact our emotions, health and finances.

Once we get our relationships moving in a direction, their impact can really pick up steam.

For this bucket, I source my intentions through admiration, partnership and curiosity. I make it a point to connect with people I admire.

Why do I admire them?

What are their values?

How do they get the most out of their life?

These are questions I ask myself when I name an intention. I also look for opportunities to invest in people. Long ago, I subscribed to the idea that we get out what we put in. This theory applies to my relationships and I consciously think of how I might partner with someone for mutual benefit.

How can I help this person?

How are we aligned?

What might we do together?

Coaches make great partners and are examples of the most intentional of relationships. Personal trainers, instructors and life coaches are all a part of my world. Each represents a powerful relationship in my life. The motivation and education I receive from them is well worth the investment. Finally, *who do I want to get to know more?* Genuine curiosity often drives me toward new relationships or reconnecting with acquaintances.

Take my friend Greg for example. I hadn't spoken to him in six months. We were introduced by a mutual contact and we had spent enough time together to realize we might make good friends. He had texted my wife and I several times to grab dinner or attend a party. Unfortunately the timing never seemed to work out. This is a person I was genuinely interested in getting to know more and I hadn't spoken to him all year. One week, I wrote in my guide I was going to drive to LA and meet him at his office. We were both in between meetings and managed to walk together for a half hour. It was great. He asked about my book and I found out he had just bought his first house. Our time together was brief but it made a big impact. A couple weeks later he invited my wife and I to go camping. We already had plans to travel out of town so I am really glad I made the trip to his office.

We all have a Greg in our lives. Taking time to improve our relationships can seem daunting. It does not have to be. Begin by connecting or reconnecting with one person. Write down an intention to call that person or grab coffee together:

E.g. Grab coffee with Jess this week

You can also record additional intentions using the included weekly guide. Plan to send flowers to your mom or a package to that friend you know is going through a rough patch.

The last item I will mention regarding the Relationship Bucket is what I call unconditional gifts. An unconditional gift is like that package you just sent. It is probably inexpensive and simple but hugely impactful. It is sometimes given to the most unsuspecting of contacts. In fact, they may be so unsuspecting that we get a weird look or odd response after our gift is received.

I recently sent a copy of *How to Change Your Mind* by Michael Pollan along with a jar of chili oil to a former coworker who lives in Boise. While he responded positively with a texted photo of his new treasures, I am sure he thought to himself, "What the heck has gotten into Bobby?" The answer has nothing to do with me and everything to do with him. He deserves to remember he is important to all kinds of people including a guy a few states away he hasn't spoken to in years. We all deserve that and interactions like that do more for all of us than we think.

Relationship Bucket Examples:
Send mom "just because" flowers
Meet Sony for sushi
Grab a coffee with Ryan V

Your intention is:

To play. Play music, play with your food or play with a friend.

The world wants you to have fun.

My left eye squints open. I can tell immediately it is early, most likely before five. I slept well and am hoping I can get another thirty minutes of sleep. Then a thought rolls in that I cannot shake. I think about the power of commitment and how it enhances people, ideas and relationships. It adds strength, confidence and resilience. Commitment yields magic. I jump out of bed to follow the thought onto a page in my journal.

It is 4:47 AM when I sit on my living room couch to begin writing. I record the word "magic" first. It feels like the right thing I am after. I think about all the magic that comes into my life through commitment, magic like resources, opportunities and growth. I also think how challenging commitment can be, and how consistency escapes me. "There is something to this," I think.

I pen the first few sentences of a poem sitting in darkness. The kitchen ceiling light spills into the living room and illuminates my journal just enough. I hear morning. Newport Boulevard's early traffic creates faint, intermittent noise a couple blocks away. Occasional wind gusts pass by whistling a tune. I also hear pen on paper.

What starts as nothing more than a curious recognition develops into six stanzas. I include listening, forgiveness and love as other sources of magic. I also manage to rhyme enough to convey the sound buzzing in my head. Just after six, I shut my journal, grab my shoes and head to the beach. I need to run.

In the previous section, I mention how impactful relationships can be to our lives. Our creativity can be just as impactful. Writing "The Magic" on that Saturday morning added to my creativity. Searching for the right words, organizing each stanza and rhyming words was a mental workout; a creativity practice. That poem served as my first motivation to practice The 5 Buckets and write this book.

Increasing our creativity can be like adding rocket fuel to our lives. And that fuel can jet us to the moon, Jupiter, another galaxy... wherever. Creativity is powerful stuff. Unfortunately, most of us think creativity is something we are born with or that falls into our lap from time to time. It is neither.

I regularly read a blog by James Altucher and he once wrote about our "idea muscle." He states, "If we do not exercise our idea muscle every day it will atrophy and we lose our ability to be creative." It is a message that resonates with me and I have since explored many ways to build my own creative muscles. Creativity is something to be nurtured and once activated, can produce remarkable effects.

Think about other ways to work out our creative muscles. There is one, centuries-old, purpose-built and battle-tested technique for increasing our creative strength: play. Play is an on-ramp to imagination, invention and expression. It is a universal language we have used since we were able to walk up to other children and say, "Let's do this." It is through play I discovered my love for sport, writing, cooking, travel and people. The best part about play is that it lacks restrictions and expectations. We do not fixate on the approach nor the outcome of it. There is a flexibility with play that allows us to experiment, enjoy and progress.

Ever since I can remember I have been intimidated by the kitchen. I lacked confidence in my ability to cook a meal or even whip together anything more complicated than a sandwich. That is until I discovered my sense of play in the kitchen. I was watching an episode of *Make This Tonight* when Kristen Kish pulled out a chef's torch to smoke some yogurt for a dish she was making. I was mesmerized by how she calmly worked with this fire pistol to brown edges and light hickory wood chips.

I immediately rushed to Sur La Table and swooped up my own torch. Just opening the package gave me fits. It seemed impossible that I was going to be able to use such a device with any sort of confidence. But my desire to play prevailed. I tossed aside my anxiety and lit up some wood chips of my own. I organized them into a foil boat I formed with my fingers, then placed the boat next to some vegetables in my Dutch oven. I leveraged Kristin's instructions to smoke organic carrots, beets and yogurt right there on my kitchen countertop. It was awesome. And while the smoked veg was delicious, I wasn't winning culinary awards anytime soon. It did however, unlock something inside me.

What started out as play with a chef's torch morphed into understanding, confidence and capability. Now, I mess around in the kitchen every day. I am convinced my experiments there seed expansion and enhancement across the rest of my world. My work inside the kitchen improves my work outside the kitchen.

In a subtle way, those smoked vegetables represent a little bit of genius. Not my genius but a genius I stumbled upon through the combination of Kristen's instruction, the chef's torch and my own determination. This type of genius appears all the time but perhaps its subtlety keeps us from celebrating it and replicating it.

As mentioned in the introduction, I attended a retreat near Idyllwild with some friends. A core theme of the weekend was to challenge ourselves to create music. A few of the leaders are avid players of the didgeridoo (yep, that weird Australian woodwind we all learned about in middle school) and brought several to the retreat for us to play. While most of us struggled to create any substantial sound, my friend Kenny could make these things roar. He hadn't been playing it much longer than any of us but the dude just rocked it. I was blown away by what I was seeing from my good friend. Kenny is a successful entrepreneur, former college athlete and simply stated, not "the didgeridoo type" at least so I thought. But here he was slaying the didge like an Aboriginal master. At one point, I actually had a remarkable vision of Kenny playing in front of thousands of people. "I'm telling you, they will come from miles away!" I said convincingly. It was one of the more genius moments I had witnessed in a long while and proves they can be found in the oddest places or the most obscure of instruments.

Creativity provides us invention. It serves as our superpower. With it, we have the ability to navigate our biggest challenges and explore our greatest opportunities. But creativity is a knife that needs to be sharpened. Superman weakens from kryptonite; creativity weakens from neglect. Write down one creative intention. Writing, drawing and coloring are all easy favorites to get rolling:

E.g. Journal for 20 minutes this week

**This represents one creative moment you get to experience and can be whatever you choose.
It is your moment to play, design, build and enjoy.**

What a wonderful opportunity.

A short time ago I sent my mom "just because" flowers. It was one of my intentions. The flowers arrived in a box. It was a tropical bouquet including red ginger and some bright greens. They had shipped all the way from Ecuador so they needed a little love once she received them. My mom cleaned a vase, clipped the stems and added some additional greenery from her garden. She smelled each flower and placed them gently into the vase. She took her time making sure it all looked just right. My gift became her small creation. She later texted me a picture of her beautiful arrangement. She also called to tell me how much she enjoyed putting it together. She had forgotten how much she liked that feeling. This is a good example of how even the simplest of moments can spark our creativity and sense of accomplishment.

Creativity Bucket Examples:
Play the ukulele for 30 minutes
Write for 40 minutes
Color with Scarlett

Your intention is:

✦ *To nourish. Nourish yourself with gifts*
of good food, good thoughts
and good movement.

The world wants you well.

I say goodbye to Ken and put AirPods into my ears. I click the "Liked Songs" section of Spotify on my phone. "Whenever You're Ready" by Boston Bun plays. The sun begins to set a half mile in front of me. I head to the beach to see if I can finish a run before the sun completely disappears.

When I arrive at the boardwalk, I sit on a bench to take off my shoes. I plan to run north on the sand. I will turn around once I hit the Santa Ana River inlet. The trip totals just over four miles and is a run I've done several times in the past few months.

I pass by Lifeguard Tower 40 and the sun is almost down. It is an insane sunset. Orange, pink and red streaks cover the sky. The shadows of sailboats and yachts break up the remarkable skyline. Other people stare at the sight as I run behind them.

The temperature might be below fifty degrees. The cold sand feels good on my feet. I also like the challenge of keeping balance and finding tire lines to follow; a lifeguard truck must've passed through just minutes prior. Every step feels different from the next. Even though I've run this stretch of beach before, in many ways, it feels like my first time.

The brisk Pacific air fuels each inhale. I take paced, deep breaths. I enjoy each one.

As planned, I turn around at the river. Only a sliver of sunlight remains. A fingernail of a moon shines above my head and on my right. I can still make out the surf from the moon's reflection. Otherwise I have trouble seeing just twenty feet in front of me. The environment is different from my morning runs. I appreciate the difference.

As I near the end, I think about how thankful I am for the experience. How I am lucky enough to live by such a beautiful place. How I am healthy enough to complete a four-mile run on the sand. I stop at Tower 32. Back where I started. I look out at the dark, limitless Pacific and take one last deep breath, then say to myself, "Thank you."

Our health is critical to maximizing our intentioned life. It represents a way of enhancing and maintaining the vehicle for our journey. We need clean lungs to breathe deeply, strong hearts to fuel our body and sharp senses to take it all in. Self-care anchors the other areas of our lives.

The Health Bucket gets a lot of attention as the health and fitness market is worth roughly $30 billion in the United States alone. Unfortunately, our obesity epidemic also costs us $150 billion in healthcare costs annually. Additionally, The World Health Organization estimates mental health conditions cost us over $1 trillion per year globally. The WHO also notes people living with mental health conditions are more likely to face other physical health problems, causing early mortality of ten to twenty years.

While this information might be intimidating, I find a little effort goes a long way. The tiniest of intentions can drastically impact this bucket. The intentions regarding my health also represent some of my most enjoyable, whether it be basking in sunshine while on a long walk, listening to that perfect song while on a bike ride or taking a moment to notice my body breathe and pulse while I meditate.

What is one health intention you might enjoy this week? Take a minute to think then record it here:

E.g. Do 30 minutes of yoga at the nearby park

_____

Let's return to my experience in the kitchen to illustrate how small intentions in this bucket can lead to substantial impacts. One of my first intentions for my Health Bucket was a 2-for-1* to cook a meal for my wife (*Relationship plus Health - see Tips, Tricks and Suggestions for further explanation). Since I was going to take the time to cook a meal, I was going to make certain it was healthy. As mentioned previously, cooking at this point was a big challenge for me so I wanted a large payoff which I feel I ultimately received.

I went to the grocery store on my way home from work to grab the items necessary to cook my meal. I was following a vegan recipe off the internet so I needed a good amount of produce and some items like vegan cheese I knew we didn't already have. I enjoyed the experience of shopping with purpose. I also bought a few other items in my quest for "a healthier me" that I'll mention in a bit. I put a plan in place, executed it and came away satisfied. After my personal grocery store adventure, I cooked something healthy for myself and surprised my wife through one, simple intention.

There were secondary impacts from this experience that struck me as well. Because I bought extra produce, I sliced and stored them for other meals and snacks. I had also picked up some tea during my grocery visit as I was interested in having tea before bed to help me sleep. Not only did I prepare tea that night but I did so many nights following. My comfort and curiosity in the kitchen expanded quickly from preparing that initial meal. Lastly, my newfound tea habit curbed my craving for snacks and alcohol after dinner. Ultimately, that first meal led to several benefits I hadn't originally considered.

Subtraction through addition is another interesting strategy I implement with my health. I used to correlate being healthier with limiting oneself in some way (stop smoking, eat less red meat, don't drink alcohol, etc.). I have noticed that by *adding* three intentions for a week, less healthy actions seem to fall away more naturally. I am also surprised by how my more creative intentions make it easier for me to do my more recurring intentions. If I take a long, morning beach walk with a friend then I find it easier to hit the gym in the afternoon. If I surround myself with healthy fruit, I tend to crave less sweets.

I mentioned earlier that our health anchors the other areas of our lives. When I am deliberate with my health choices, I find it much easier to explore other areas with confidence and curiosity. I can do better work, am more creative and more aware of good opportunities. I recommend balancing health intentions across food, physical activity and meditation. Since I tend to over index on activity, I make a point to listen to a guided meditation or prepare a healthy snack each week.

I'll finish this section with a short story about my good friend, Cameron. Not that long ago, Cameron and I began walking together. Now at first,

I am not even sure we planned each walk as a healthy intention but more as a friendly visit. Cameron showed up in jeans and a button-down shirt to further illustrate this observation. What started as a short, conversational walk around my neighborhood turned into a weekly routine. Cameron also began walking on his own and with other people. At times, he would walk for over twelve miles during a single trip! Within six weeks, I noticed a big change in his appearance and his attitude. He had clearly gotten a ton out of his activity and it all literally started from taking a few, small steps forward. What small steps might you take this week?

Health Bucket Examples:

Walk for 30 minutes with Cameron
(2-for-1 Health plus Relationships)
Meditate with WakingUp app for 20 minutes
Bike ride around Back Bay for an hour

Your intention is:

To listen. Listen to your peers, your elders, your heroes and your heart.

The world wants to share with you.

I lie about my couch, taking in the morning. My feet are reclined and cold from Pacific winds drafting through my home. I read *The Right to Write* by Julia Cameron while my coffee brews.

I stare out our double glass doors watching the neighborhood rise. Across the street, Buzz hangs a "Merry Christmas" sign beside his entry door. It looks out of place. The red and white clash with the weathered cream stucco of his canalside home. Car engines start and birds chirp. The sounds blend together forming an almost pleasant tune, deafened just enough by the glass doors.

I enjoy reading again and can't do it enough. Julia really works for me. I do wish her book had longer chapters. After each one, she suggests a writing exercise. I sense I can't keep up. I finish the chapter and the bottom of the page reads:

Set aside fifteen minutes. Writing longhand, describe a situation in your life that you are currently trying to metabolize.

As I read Julia's instructions, the *Student of Intention* podcast comes to mind. I am excited to create it and also scared. I imagine I'll share what I learn while writing this book. But I need to learn the medium and bring my personality to it. I need to bring stories. I want to produce compelling, professional content. It is another step forward for my creative pursuits. My goal is to write more books, build a community and help that community thrive. I am clear on those drivers.

I am grateful for this morning. It reminds me what I am living for: quiet and well-paced mornings to myself. I chug along stretching, reading and writing. Little chores introduce me to the day's happenings. I put away tea cups from last night, juice some celery for when Tracy wakes, grind my coffee and hang with Julia.

This is living with intention.

If our health anchors the other areas of our life, learning expands those areas and changes their possibilities.

Learning provides us perspective.
We learn more about the lives we want to live
and can better serve our purpose.

Business and personal growth books were the first forms of literature to really hook me. From *Good to Great* to *The Happiness Advantage* to *Grit*, I can't get enough of them. Each time I read or listen to one of these works, I borrow a lens with which to view the world. I distinctly notice my perspective shift while enjoying *Shoe Dog* or *The War of Art*. It's a remarkable experience and I love the feeling. So when I began focusing on my own Learning Bucket, I started with these books. I bought a copy of *The Alchemist* from Amazon and jumped in right away. Paulo Coelho's words of omens, Personal Legends and The Universe conspiring to help the shepherd energized my mind as I ran my business and began writing this book. Reading almost always serves as an intention in my Learning Bucket each week.

When I think of learning, I envision diving into a hardcover book. But we live in a new world where digital content is everywhere. Never before have we had such access to vast selections of music, movies, books, articles, videos, speeches, tutorials, lessons, shows and classes. Stay-at-home parents are learning how to build e-commerce empires, reformed prisoners are coding software after weeks of online training and children are becoming culinary masters from watching YouTube. With the right focus, a quality laptop and solid internet connection can stand up to just about any form of traditional education.

We live in a time almost perfectly suited to help us self-educate. And at the same time, new, evolving challenges exist. The same content that can help inspire and teach us can just as easily distract and overwhelm us.

Screens and streams surround our minds in ways they're not necessarily equipped to handle. We face a daily onslaught of digital advertisements, messages and notifications jockeying for our attention. And while little friction prohibits consuming mass amounts of content, it remains difficult to retain and apply information we ingest. I am fascinated by this bucket as it is often the most perplexing of the five.

When I sit down to name my intentions, thinking about what I want to learn consistently takes the most time. The book I am reading tends to occupy one intention and I have to do a bit of research to identify the other two. Podcasts are a favorite medium of mine, particularly if I can listen to them during a drive. Unfortunately, I subscribe almost entirely to sports pods like Bill Simmons' and Ryen Russillo's. While I enjoy Colin Cowherd's take on what makes a great quarterback, it's not the type of audio that warrants Learning Bucket consideration. *TED Talks Daily*, *The James Altucher Show*, *Rich Roll* and *Aubrey Marcus* are a few I've tuned into for more educational purposes.

We all get loads of value from books and podcasts but my biggest academic leaps come from 1:1 instruction. Price and availability can be a challenge but it is tough to put any medium ahead of learning from another human being face to face. I am deeply entrenched in the development of my golf game alongside Chris Dunn, an instructor at Urban Golf Performance. Chris has accelerated my pace of improvement unlike any training method I've previously tried. Like most personal instructors, he caters to my strengths, weaknesses and personality, and challenges my work ethic. This enables efficient and expansive growth combined with a bit of relationship building. I consider Chris a friend I will remain connected to long after he's done teaching me how to flatten out the trajectory of my pitching wedge. The next best thing to in-person lessons are 1:1 lessons online. The combination of platforms like Instagram and Zoom make it remarkably effective to connect with all kinds of instructors at a relatively low cost. We get customized, personal experience essentially anytime and anywhere. Take advantage of this shift and find an instructor to help fill the Learning Bucket in the coming weeks.

What might you learn this week? Record an intention here:

E.g. Watch a YouTube video on how to be a more confident public speaker

---

I close this section with how it began: learning from Julia. In the same book, she describes an idea of stealing time:

> **"If we learn to write from the sheer love of writing, there is always enough time, but time must be stolen like a quick kiss between lovers on the run. As a shrewd woman once told me, "The busiest and most important man can always find time for you if he's in love with you and, if he can't, then he is not in love." When we love our writing, we find time for it."**

I love her simile of stealing a quick kiss. What a cool way to write about grabbing time by the collar. I also subscribe to her idea that if we love something enough, we find time for it. If we figure out what moments we want to experience, then we'll find time for them.

Much of living with intention revolves around this idea. With that, Julia is as much an author of this book as I. Steven, Wayne, Jay, Joseph, Bill and

Elizabeth too. They are my partners. Every word of theirs I read connects us. We build a relationship across time, experience and space. Their wisdom expands my perspective and ability to explore.

Like the rest of the buckets, learning is a practice best completed in pursuit of joy and not knowledge. I don't know what lessons I'm going to pick up each time I read *The Soul of Money* or *Turning Pro*. And I don't want to. Instead, I show up, listen and enjoy. Do it enough and the knowledge comes.

Learning Bucket Examples:
Read one chapter in The Lean Startup
Listen to lessons by Eckhart Tolle for 20 minutes
Google how to replace my porch light fixture

Your intention is:

To build. Build for yourself
then build for the rest of us.

The world awaits your offering.

Since the pandemic hit, my workspace resides in our guestroom. Being in the back of our home, I am shielded from neighborhood noise. It is a painfully quiet space. I hear occasional floor squeaks from the neighbors above, but otherwise it's just thoughts and keyboard strokes.

Sitting at my desk, I pry open my laptop. The desk is small and tucked into the corner left of entry. I sit on a short, wheeled stool, the kind a doctor might sit on during a physical. I bought it because I've always liked those stools.

I have a medium-sized project to tackle. It is a denser intention than normal. I want to create an incentive plan for a client; a way for their employees to earn bonuses. This is specifically for their customer success team.

I break down the project into a beginning, middle and end. I attach a question to each part:

Goal (Beginning) - *Why are we doing this?*
Structure (Middle) - *How do we do this?*
Payment Details (End) - *What happens when we do this?*

I record this on a Google Doc. Getting just these twenty-three words onto the screen sparks my next hour of work. I enjoy filling out the blank space and discovering how each section leads into the other. I re-read each word as how I imagine a stranger might read them, without my perspective adding context and narrowing focus.

Once complete, I email the Doc to my client for review. I schedule time to share and gather feedback. I am happy with the progress and look forward to the meeting.

Before I practiced The 5 Buckets and named work intentions, I did not recall work projects so clearly. I certainly did not appreciate them the way I do now. I thought of such an example as more of a task. Something to be done. A means to an end. Now I explore the nuance of the process. I appreciate the discovery taking place, the creativity I bring to the project and the uniqueness of my approach, in that moment, at that time.

Work examples like this one are not the sole focus of the Work Bucket. Consider chores, volunteer work, side hustles and service of any kind. It all can be broken down into a beginning, middle and end. It can all be enjoyed. Gratitude is key.

Setting work intentions each week is not a productivity practice. It is not intended to offer shortcuts or organizational gains. Enjoyment of work's process is our aim.

Whether we are clearing a corner of the garage or preparing a presentation for our boss, gratitude for the experience is the goal.

Remember, an intention is a planned moment we want to experience. Work experiences are no different. We choose the work we do.

What is one work intention you choose to do this week? Consider how you might be grateful for the experience before recording it here:

E.g. Create onboarding process to help new team members ramp up faster

✎ _____

Reflection is a key component to all the buckets but especially work. Estimates suggest we spend ninety thousand hours of our lives doing work. With so many hours dedicated to work, it is challenging to identify and appreciate its small, daily moments. But it's also that much more imperative. Reflect with purpose. Do not simply dwell on the positive or negative outcomes. Think about how you showed up to your intentions; your chosen moments. Consider what you learn, how they served you and how they served others.

This book aims at increasing your ability to live with intention. Doing so across all facets of life ultimately enables you to enjoy and create more beautiful work. Deeper relationships open opportunities and alignment. Training your creative muscles helps you add unique value quickly. A healthy mind and body provide positivity and energy. The more you learn, the more perspective and skills you can bring to your work.

As I practice The 5 Buckets, my work becomes increasingly more important to me. I do not mention this lightly. My work has always been part of my identity, part of how others see me and how I see myself. By "more important,"

**I mean I better realize the value of my work
and the time I spend doing it.**

I understand how it impacts the other areas of my life. I understand how it can impact other people, and how I can increase or decrease these impacts.

This understanding played a major role in my writing this book, starting a community and exploring other creative pursuits. As I write this page, I am still learning. I am still figuring it out. But there is something to it. It is worth taking for a walk and pulling further on the thread.

Work Bucket Examples:
Lead a training session for a new product
Clean the front patio
*Gather revenue and expenses to estimate
year-end tax bill*

HOW TO BEGIN

John and I sip coffee outside C'est Si Bon Bakery. It is a few minutes after seven. We arrived just as they opened. People hurry past us to the front door in search of coffee and croissants.

He and his wife returned from a holiday trip to Costa Rica just days earlier. He is rejuvenated, tan and full of energy. He shares ideas from the seven books he read during his stay. He mentions he only woke to an alarm a few times. Otherwise he slept freely for ten hours each night. He also ran on the beach most days. I can tell he enjoyed the trip.

Then he turns to me and asks, "How is the book coming?"

John and I had talked about The 5 Buckets a few times before he left for his trip. During one of our conversations, he asked me to think about what is possible if I complete the book. He knew how the framework had helped me. He wanted to know what it might do for other people.

"I'm trying to write the conclusion. I think it's almost finished," I respond.

It is in that conversation I best define living with intention. I define it as enjoying the pursuit of purpose. And I want to give this experience to other people.

I want to help you enjoy the pursuit of purpose.

I want you to find excitement in the everyday. To read more Elizabeth Gilbert. To explore your neighborhood on foot. To call your sister or your brother or your friend from school. To slice up a pineapple for breakfast. To write a poem about your first kiss. To play a jaw harp. To clean the patio. I want you to do it all, and savor every bit of it.

John then asks of enjoying the pursuit of purpose, "How do people begin?"

Begin by giving yourself space, space to think about what you've always wanted to learn or create. Think about who you want to connect with or who wants to hear from you. Think about the healthy gifts you can give your mind and body. Think about what you can contribute through work, volunteering or at home. Then think about a small experience associated with one of these thoughts. Think of a little step forward you might take.

Now, write it down. Write it in the Intention Guide, a journal or on the back of an electric bill you received in the mail. It doesn't matter. Write it and tell yourself how you want to spend a single moment of your time.

Then act.

**The pursuit of purpose comprises three parts:
Action, Discovery and Alignment.**

Action is showing up to the party: getting out of bed, off the couch and into the world.

You take the walk, go for the run, swim, bike, dance or lift.

You create the presentation, outline the book, write the song, take the class or meet the mentor.

Taking action is a practice. Develop your practice and **Discovery** comes.

You discover your awareness of where you want to go, who you want to be and what you want to create. New, interesting and compelling paths present themselves.

**Your calling calls.
And it screams louder the more you act.**

Then comes **Alignment**. As you steer your actions toward purpose, The Universe understands how to assist your pursuit. Your actions and The Universe align.

Resources and opportunities surface. Helpful relationships make themselves available.

Forces join your cause as you begin to work in flow with The Universe. Remember the words of Steven Pressfield and Wayne Dyer. These forces are strong and reinforce your effort.

If all of this still has you stalling, then take some time to think about a recent moment you've already experienced.

What did you enjoy about the moment?

How did it serve you?

Finding gratitude for life's small moments is a key to living with intention. It may even be *the* key.

By doing so, you better understand what you are getting and giving in your decisions. You see nuance and realize the stakes of how you spend your time. Like a muscle, your awareness grows stronger. You learn what moments matter and what you want to experience more often. You also gain appreciation for what just *is*.

Understand that where you are now is exactly where you are supposed to be. The 5 Buckets is not a framework for getting somewhere else. It is not a productivity practice or a goal-setting exercise. It is not meant to lead to instant success or gratification. Be wary of setting such expectations.

But realize there is magic in this simple practice. When you have an off day, write down your intentions. As you encounter challenges, write down your intentions. When you feel sidetracked, beaten or unmotivated, write down your intentions.

Just before finishing this manuscript, I sit at my guest bedroom desk feeling confused. I am in the best health of my life. I haven't drank a drop of alcohol in several months. I started a newsletter, a podcast and connected with loads of helpful people. My relationship with my wife is flourishing. I have the support of friends, family and acquaintances. And yet, I sit here wrestling feelings of doubt. Fear, anxiety and uncertainty creep into my mind.

I pull out my journal and look at last week's intentions. I read that I met up with an old friend for coffee. He had reached out to me on LinkedIn. We hadn't seen each other in over five years. I remember his smile when we greeted each other. He was so thankful I had made the time.

I read about recording my first music show with my friend, Chris. I remember listening to the different songs in his studio. We recorded our conversation, a poem and several stories between each track. It was exciting and nerve-racking. Peaceful and challenging. Chris said it was the first time he'd sat and listened to new music in a long time. He thanked me for including him in the experience.

I read about the vegan butternut squash soup I made from scratch. Slicing the squash wasn't easy but I enjoyed it. I roasted it in the oven before adding it to a big gray pot. I sauteed garlic and onions then tossed them into the pot as well. I sliced and added an apple and a couple carrots, followed by cinnamon, nutmeg, salt, pepper and vegetable stock. The soup tasted wonderful.

My doubts subside. I am enjoying the pursuit of purpose. I write down my intentions for this week. I think I'll make a mushroom soup and ride my bike to the pier with Kevin. Tracy and I will clean up the north end of the beach. We saw trash pile up on the shore the last time we were there. We'll fill up a few black trash bags. It's a small effort but it's a start.

And that's how you begin.

Don't wait. Start small. Learn as you go.

TIPS, TRICKS AND SUGGESTIONS

We are at the point in your journey where you have a framework to help you actualize the life you want. If you haven't already, I suggest jumping to the Intention Guide to record a week's worth of intentions.

When organizing my own life using The 5 Buckets, I learned a few other items worth keeping in mind as you continue your journey.

Subtraction by way of addition: This framework is all about prioritizing moments you want to experience. When naming intentions, focus on what you want to bring into your life. Do not focus on what you want to restrict from your life. When you flood your days with these moments, other parts will naturally fall off.

2-for-1s: There are times when it makes sense to slot a single intention across two buckets. Perhaps I go jogging with a friend (Health plus Relationship) or take a course on digital marketing (Learning plus Work). Or my favorite, find a new recipe to cook something special for my wife

(Creative plus Relationship). Whatever the case, there are plenty of opportunities. My only caution is to keep these to a minimum. Our goal isn't to maximize efficiency and limit our number of intentions. Our goal is to enjoy each moment we create for ourselves. Each represents a small part of the life we want to live.

Limit a recurring intention to three weeks in a row: After taking several morning rides on my road bike, it became a habit. I am going to do it anyway so I no longer feel the need to slot it as an intention in my Health Bucket. This provides room for a morning meditation or midday juicing. Whenever possible, we want to use our intentions to add something creative and specific to our lives. We want to enjoy and reflect on how each impacts us. Positive habits are awesome and something we all strive to create. Separating these habits from our intentions is also a helpful practice.

Name then schedule: As you take time and space to plan your week, name your intentions first by writing them in the included Intention Guide. It is important to do this before inputting them into a calendar. This is not a hurried exercise and our aim should be to enjoy thinking about our week ahead using a creative framework. *What do I want to learn? What have I always wanted to try? Who am I interested in reconnecting with?* Leveraging our week to provide answers to these questions can be fulfilling. After we name our intentions, schedule time to complete them. Use weekends and the early morning. I find these times particularly useful.

Replacing and awareness: The more I use The 5 Buckets, the more aware I become of my actions. One day I was visiting my cousin and his daughter, Scarlett, during their beach vacation. She and I began building a sand castle. I helped dig a massive moat around the castle to capture the crashing waves. Then I added a huge tower using her biggest toy mold. She loved my additions to her creation. It was a wonderful experience and a worthwhile intention. Later that day, I slotted that moment in as a Creative and Relationship 2-for-1. This is an example where it makes sense to replace an intention. This will happen and we should recognize these special moments. There is no need to fixate on a rigid plan. There is room to create and explore. We are learning as we go.

THE INTENTION GUIDE

Thank you for joining me in my goal of living with balance and intention. I am including a guide formatted in the same way I organize myself each week. If you take only one thing from reading this book, take a start. Begin. During my own experience using this framework, I have explored, succeeded and stumbled. When I face an obstacle, I overcome it through action. When I find momentum, I nurture it through reflection. We can be creative and efficient but above all else, we must begin.

> ## "Action is the food and drink which will nourish my success."
>
> —Og Mandino, *The Greatest Salesman in the World*

Every Sunday, I write my intentions down then schedule time to complete them in my Google calendar. You will find what system works for you.

Feeling extra intentional?
Please check out my Student of Intention newsletter,
podcast and community at
www.studentofintention.com.

I continue my quest to create the life I want one moment at a time and invite you to begin yours as well. May you get what you want from this day, this book and this life. Thank you for letting me be a small part of your adventure.

THE 5 BUCKETS

Weekly Intention Guide

Living with intention lets the universe know what we want.
As we learned long ago, actions speak louder than words.

HOW TO USE THIS GUIDE:

Record three intentions per bucket to schedule and
complete each week for twelve weeks.

An intention is a planned moment you want to experience.
The description you choose can be as brief or thorough
as necessary.

It is your opportunity to think through what moments
you want to experience during your week of life.

Be creative, be efficient and enjoy the time
you commit to the practice.

Don't wait. Start small. Learn as you go.

Week: 1 / 12
Relationships

Your support and greatest enhancers in life.

_____

_____

_____

Creativity

Hone your ability to invent, navigate and explore.

_____

_____

_____

Learning

Gain perspective. Better serve your purpose.

_____

_____

_____

Health

Maintain the vehicle for your journey.

_____

_____

_____

Work

Your contribution. Add treasure to the world.

_____

_____

_____

> # "Growth is an erratic forward movement: two steps forward, one step back. Remember that and be very gentle with yourself."

Julia Cameron

Weekly Reflection:

Record an observation regarding three intentions from the previous week. What did you enjoy? What did you most avoid? Recall how the week played out.

_____

_____

_____

_____

_____

Week: 2 / 12

Relationships

Your support and greatest enhancers in life.

_____

_____

_____

Creativity

Hone your ability to invent, navigate and explore.

_____

_____

_____

Learning

Gain perspective. Better serve your purpose.

_____

_____

_____

Health

Maintain the vehicle for your journey.

_____

_____

_____

Work

Your contribution. Add treasure to the world.

_____

_____

_____

"The only way to make sense out of change is to plunge into it, move with it, and join the dance."

Alan Watts

Weekly Reflection:

Record an observation regarding three intentions from the previous week. What did you enjoy? What did you most avoid? Recall how the week played out.

_____

_____

_____

_____

_____

Week: 3 / 12

Relationships

Your support and greatest enhancers in life.

_____

_____

_____

Creativity

Hone your ability to invent, navigate and explore.

_____

_____

_____

Learning

Gain perspective. Better serve your purpose.

_____

_____

_____

Health

Maintain the vehicle for your journey.

_____

_____

_____

Work

Your contribution. Add treasure to the world.

_____

_____

_____

> # "Life is not a problem to be solved, but a reality to be experienced."

Soren Kierkegaard

Weekly Reflection:

Record an observation regarding three intentions from the previous week. What did you enjoy? What did you most avoid? Recall how the week played out.

_____

_____

_____

_____

Week: 4 / 12

Relationships

Your support and greatest enhancers in life.

_____

_____

_____

Creativity

Hone your ability to invent, navigate and explore.

_____

_____

_____

Learning

Gain perspective. Better serve your purpose.

_____

_____

_____

Health

Maintain the vehicle for your journey.

_____

_____

_____

Work

Your contribution. Add treasure to the world.

_____

_____

_____

> # "I can do nothing for you but work on myself... you can do nothing for me but work on yourself!"

Ram Dass

Weekly Reflection:

Record an observation regarding three intentions from the previous week. What did you enjoy? What did you most avoid? Recall how the week played out.

_____

_____

_____

_____

Week: 5 / 12

Relationships

Your support and greatest enhancers in life.

_____

_____

Creativity

Hone your ability to invent, navigate and explore.

_____

_____

Learning

Gain perspective. Better serve your purpose.

_____

_____

Health

Maintain the vehicle for your journey.

_____

_____

Work

Your contribution. Add treasure to the world.

_____

_____

_____

> **"Respond to every call that excites your spirit."**

Rumi

Weekly Reflection:

Record an observation regarding three intentions from the previous week. What did you enjoy? What did you most avoid? Recall how the week played out.

_____

_____

_____

_____

_____

Week: 6 / 12
Relationships
Your support and greatest enhancers in life.

_____

_____

_____

Creativity
Hone your ability to invent, navigate and explore.

_____

_____

_____

Learning
Gain perspective. Better serve your purpose.

_____

_____

_____

Health
Maintain the vehicle for your journey.

_____

_____

_____

Work
Your contribution. Add treasure to the world.

_____

_____

_____

> **"The universe buries strange jewels deep within us all, and then stands back to see if we can find them."**

Elizabeth Gilbert

Weekly Reflection:

Record an observation regarding three intentions from the previous week. What did you enjoy? What did you most avoid? Recall how the week played out.

_____

_____

_____

_____

Week: 7 / 12

Relationships

Your support and greatest enhancers in life.

_____

_____

_____

Creativity

Hone your ability to invent, navigate and explore.

_____

_____

_____

Learning

Gain perspective. Better serve your purpose.

_____

_____

_____

Health

Maintain the vehicle for your journey.

_____

_____

_____

Work

Your contribution. Add treasure to the world.

_____

_____

_____

"The more scared we are of a work or calling, the more sure we can be that we have to do it."

Steven Pressfield

Weekly Reflection:

Record an observation regarding three intentions from the previous week. What did you enjoy? What did you most avoid? Recall how the week played out.

_____

_____

_____

_____

Week: 8 / 12
Relationships
Your support and greatest enhancers in life.

_____

_____

_____

Creativity
Hone your ability to invent, navigate and explore.

_____

_____

_____

Learning
Gain perspective. Better serve your purpose.

_____

_____

_____

Health
Maintain the vehicle for your journey.

_____

_____

_____

Work
Your contribution. Add treasure to the world.

_____

_____

_____

"The power of intention is the power to manifest, to create, to live a life of unlimited abundance, and to attract into your life the right people at the right moments."

Wayne Dyer

Weekly Reflection:

Record an observation regarding three intentions from the previous week. What did you enjoy? What did you most avoid? Recall how the week played out.

_____

_____

_____

_____

Week: 9 / 12

Relationships

Your support and greatest enhancers in life.

_____

_____

_____

Creativity

Hone your ability to invent, navigate and explore.

_____

_____

_____

Learning

Gain perspective. Better serve your purpose.

_____

_____

_____

Health

Maintain the vehicle for your journey.

_____

_____

_____

Work

Your contribution. Add treasure to the world.

_____

_____

_____

"What if I fall?"

"Oh, but Darling, what if you fly?"

Erin Hanson

Weekly Reflection:

Record an observation regarding three intentions from the previous week. What did you enjoy? What did you most avoid? Recall how the week played out.

_____

_____

_____

_____

Relationships

Your support and greatest enhancers in life.

_____

_____

_____

Creativity

Hone your ability to invent, navigate and explore.

_____

_____

_____

Learning

Gain perspective. Better serve your purpose.

_____

_____

_____

Health

Maintain the vehicle for your journey.

_____

_____

_____

Work

Your contribution. Add treasure to the world.

_____

_____

_____

> # "The more you move, the easier it is to keep moving. Maintain the momentum."

James Clear

Weekly Reflection:

Record an observation regarding three intentions from the previous week. What did you enjoy? What did you most avoid? Recall how the week played out.

_____

_____

_____

_____

Relationships

Your support and greatest enhancers in life.

_____

_____

Creativity

Hone your ability to invent, navigate and explore.

_____

_____

Learning

Gain perspective. Better serve your purpose.

_____

_____

Health

Maintain the vehicle for your journey.

_____

_____

Work

Your contribution. Add treasure to the world.

_____

_____

> # "Intention is one of the most powerful forces there is. What you mean when you do a thing will always determine the outcome. The law creates the world."

Brenna Yovanoff

Weekly Reflection:

Record an observation regarding three intentions from the previous week. What did you enjoy? What did you most avoid? Recall how the week played out.

_____

_____

_____

_____

_____

Week: 12 / 12

Relationships

Your support and greatest enhancers in life.

_____

_____

_____

Creativity

Hone your ability to invent, navigate and explore.

_____

_____

_____

Learning

Gain perspective. Better serve your purpose.

_____

_____

_____

Health

Maintain the vehicle for your journey.

_____

_____

_____

Work

Your contribution. Add treasure to the world.

_____

_____

_____

> # "Only those who will risk going too far can possibly find out how far one can go."

T. S. Eliot

Weekly Reflection:

Record an observation regarding three intentions from the previous week. What did you enjoy? What did you most avoid? Recall how the week played out.

_____

_____

_____

_____

THANK YOU

Don't wait. Start small. Learn as you go.